To Aunt Carol (Sister Kathleen O'Halloran), Sister Carol Conly, and all the Sisters of Mercy—the best by far!—EL

For Grandma Jeanne and Aunt Kaki—SK

PENGUIN WORKSHOP
An imprint of Penguin Random House LLC
1745 Broadway, New York, NY 10019
penguinrandomhouse.com

Design by Taylor Abatiell
Text set in Adobe Garamond Pro

The art was created using Photoshop.

Library of Congress Cataloging-in-Publication Data is available.

First published in the United States of America by Penguin Workshop, 2026

Manufactured in China
HH

ISBN 9798217247400
10 9 8 7 6 5 4 3 2 1

The authorized representative in the EU for product safety and compliance is Penguin Random House Ireland, Morrison Chambers, 32 Nassau Street, Dublin D02 YH68, Ireland, https://eu-contact.penguin.ie.

POPE LEO XIV

A WHO HQ ILLUSTRATED BIOGRAPHY

by
Ellen Labrecque

illustrated by
Sam Kalda

PENGUIN WORKSHOP

On May 8, 2025, the new pope—the head of the Roman Catholic Church—walked onto the balcony of St. Peter's Basilica in Vatican City. Tens of thousands of people from all over the world cheered from the square below. All popes are special, but this one was especially unique. He was the first pope from the United States! He waved to the crowd as they continued to clap and cheer. Once it became quieter, the new pope spoke in Italian. "Peace be with you all," he began.

Who was this new pope?

Popes choose a new name when they are elected. Pope Leo XIV was born Robert Francis Prevost on September 14, 1955, in Chicago, Illinois. Nicknamed Bob, he was the youngest of three children, and his two older brothers were John Joseph and Louis Martín. Bob's father, Louis Marius Prevost, was a school superintendent, and his mother, Mildred Prevost, was a school librarian.

Bob and his family lived in Dolton, a suburb of Chicago, and were members of St. Mary of the Assumption Parish. The boys also went to elementary school there. The family was very faithful and attended Mass, or church service, every Sunday as well as on religious holidays. Bob and his brothers were altar servers, the priest's helpers, during Mass, and his mom sang in the church choir.

Even as a child, Bob felt in his heart that he wanted to live a religious life. However, he still did typical kid stuff, such as cheering on his favorite baseball team, the Chicago White Sox, and playing baseball in the Little League. But he also engaged in more unique games, such as pretending to be a priest.

Bob would set up an ironing board to mimic an altar and use Necco Wafers, a type of candy, as communion wafers, which are pieces of bread that are important to Catholic Mass. "I THINK HE KNEW IT BY FIRST GRADE, THAT HE WAS GOING TO BE A PRIEST," his brother John said about Bob.

Who's Who in the Catholic Church?

The Pope: The leader of the entire Catholic Church, which has more than a billion members! He lives in Vatican City (a tiny country within Rome, Italy). This position is usually a lifelong appointment.

Cardinals: This group assists the pope in making big decisions. There are more than two hundred of them, and they vote to elect the pope.

Bishops: They are responsible for overseeing their dioceses. A diocese is a big group of churches in a particular area, like a state with a governor. There are over five thousand bishops worldwide.

Priests: They are in charge of local churches, known as parishes. A parish is one community going to one church, like a town with a mayor. Priests lead masses and also assist with essential moments in Catholics' lives, such as weddings and baptisms. Priests are called "Father" and then their name. Some priests use their first names after "Father," while others use their last names.

Nuns: Women in the Catholic Church who live in a community with other nuns and lead a life of service. They perform good works as teachers in Catholic schools or by assisting those in need. Nuns are not allowed to lead Mass.

Deacons: These men assist priests and bishops in their duties. Unlike other members of church leadership, deacons are allowed to marry.

In 1969, when Bob was fourteen, he attended St. Augustine Seminary High School, an all-boys boarding school in Holland, Michigan, approximately two hours from his home. Boys who were considering the priesthood one day went to this high school. As a student at St. Augustine, Bob sang in the choir and served as editor-in-chief of the high school yearbook.

Bob was president of his senior high school class! He also enjoyed performing in skits: In one he acted as Julius Caesar, the famous Roman general. Bob was known as the brainy kid at school. He excelled in his classes, especially in math and foreign languages, such as French. “He was known as the tutor of the school,” a former classmate said. “If you had problems with your homework, go see Prevost. . . . And Bob would help us!”

Bob chose to attend Villanova University, a Catholic institution outside of Philadelphia, Pennsylvania, for college. Villanova, like his high school, follows the mission of Saint Augustine, which, in addition to academics, emphasizes the importance of telling the truth and maintaining a good circle of friends—part of their motto is **truth**, **unity**, **and love**. These words held real meaning to Bob. He wanted to live a life helping others.

Bob majored in mathematics at Villanova and, just like in high school, was considered one of the brightest students there. He lived with other students who also planned to become priests. However, different aspects of college life sometimes did sneak in. While attending Mass, Bob often heard a guy right outside selling sandwiches hollering, "Hoagie man!" During the summers, Bob took care of a local Catholic graveyard by weeding and mowing the grass. This peaceful job allowed him ample time to think and pray while working.

Bob graduated from Villanova in 1977, at the age of twenty-one, with a degree in mathematics. He started his formal training to become a priest that same year when he joined an Augustinian church in St. Louis, Missouri. Here Bob lived as a novice, or beginner, for one year as a trial period. He lived with the religious community to decide whether he wanted to continue his path toward the priesthood. Bob loved the parish community and even played ball with kids after Sunday Mass in the local park.

Bob moved back home to Chicago after his trial year to continue his studies in religion at Catholic Theological Union, a school that teaches students to become religious leaders. Devoting his life to the priesthood was becoming increasingly real. Around this time, Bob spoke with his dad and asked if he should consider a more traditional life, such as getting married, like his father had. Bob's dad reassured his son that the path he was on was the right one for him. This conversation and reassurance eased Bob's fears. He knew he was now ready to become a priest.

Next, Bob moved to Rome, Italy, to continue his studies. In June 1982, at the age of twenty-six, he was ordained as a priest in a religious ceremony. While living in Rome, he studied the language and became a fluent Italian speaker. Bob loved taking long car rides and sang songs in Italian to practice his skills. Around this time, he met Pope John Paul II, who had been the pope for four years. Nobody knew at the time that a current pope was meeting a future pope.

In 1985, Bob moved to Peru as a missionary and priest. There, he shared his Catholic faith with people throughout the country, assisted those living in poverty, and became fluent in Spanish. This was just the work he always wanted to do. In one severe storm, people in his church lost their homes due to torrential rain. Bob did everything he could to help. "There was so much need—he got his hands dirty," recalled a fellow priest.

Bob was called Padre Roberto in Peru. When he said Mass each Sunday, he always remembered to keep his homilies, the part of the service where a priest teaches a message, short. He knew people didn't want to listen too long and thought the better way to get his message to them was to be direct. "He said that a homily should be short and to the point, like a miniskirt," one church member explained.

In 2001, after mainly living in Peru for fifteen years, Bob, now forty-six, was elected to head the Order of St. Augustine worldwide. This appointment meant he had to move to Rome but would travel extensively, visiting other Augustinian priests and communities. He still loved to go on long car rides—they gave him time to think and pray. Instead of flying to Spain from Rome, he would drive. Or he would drive from Brisbane to Sydney, Australia—an over nine-hour trip!

Bob served for twelve years as the head of the Augustinian order. He was a gentle leader who was a good listener and made sure to meet and befriend Catholics from all over the world. He made a point to meet the locals, even eating local food, such as fertilized duck eggs in the Philippines. He joked, though, that it took him three days to digest them!

In 2015, Bob was promoted again when he was named a bishop by Pope Francis, the pope at that time. Bob returned to Peru and served as a bishop there. He felt as much a Peruvian as he did an American, and in the same year, he became a citizen of Peru, too. Just as he had when he was in Peru for the first time, he went out of his way to help others. He even visited people on horseback if there were no roads for a car to get there. "He had time for everyone," said a friar who worked with Bob.

In 2023, Pope Francis called Bob back to Rome, and Bob was named a cardinal that September. One of the reasons Pope Francis named Bob a cardinal was that he felt a connection to him. They were both down-to-earth leaders who felt that serving people living in poverty and helping those in need was important. As Cardinal Prevost, Bob worked closely with Pope Francis, advising him on essential matters and appointments.

In February 2025, Pope Francis, now eighty-eight years old, became sick—his lungs and his kidneys stopped working well, and he was seriously ill over the next couple of months. Bob led the rosary, a special Catholic series of prayers with beads, in St. Peter's Square, praying for the pope's health.

Pope Francis died on April 21, 2025. A new pope now had to be selected. The papal conclave, the meeting to choose a new pope, began on May 7, with 133 cardinals, including Bob, in attendance. The conclave at the Sistine Chapel in Vatican City was highly secretive, and the cardinals would not emerge until they agreed on a new pope.

For a new pope to be selected, a cardinal needed a two-thirds majority, so this time, the winner required eighty-nine votes. At the end of the first day of the conclave, black smoke came out of the chimney of the Sistine Chapel—black smoke meant the cardinals had not selected a new pope. On the second day, after a fourth round of voting, white smoke appeared out of the chimney. A new pope was named, and it was Bob!

How Is a New Pope Chosen?

When a pope dies, the Catholic Church selects a new one through a special process called a conclave. First, cardinals from around the world gather at the Sistine Chapel in Vatican City. The number of voting cardinals varies, but when Pope Leo XIV was elected, there were 133. The cardinals don't leave, use their cell phones, or talk to anyone outside of the conclave until a new pope is selected. The cardinals vote in secret, using paper ballots. For a new cardinal to become the pope, he needs at least two-thirds of the votes. After each round of voting, the ballots are burned. If no pope is chosen, black smoke rises from the chimney. If a new pope is chosen, white smoke rises! This signals to the people watching in the square that a decision has been made. Once there is a winner, he chooses a new name. He then appears on the balcony and waves to the crowd as the new leader of the church.

Bob, at age sixty-nine, was voted the new pope for many reasons: He speaks many different languages, which is important as a pope. He also has a deep love for people experiencing poverty, having lived and worked all over the world, yet is equally at home in Rome. Bob chose Pope Leo XIV as his new name. The number behind the name means he is the fourteenth pope to choose Leo. Bob chose the name because of Pope Leo XIII (1810–1903), who fought for the rights of workers and those in need. BOB HAD SPENT HIS PRIESTHOOD FIGHTING FOR THESE RIGHTS AS WELL AND CHOSE THE NAME TO SHOW HE PLANNED TO CONTINUE DOING SO.

Pope Leo XIV became the first pope from the United States, the first Peruvian pope, and also the first pope from the Order of St. Augustine. Because he has traveled and lived extensively around the world, Pope Leo XIV speaks English, Italian, French, Spanish, and Portuguese. Pope Leo has devoted much of his time to helping those who need it the most. That has been his life's mission, and one he hopes to continue as the pope.

When a new pope is elected, Catholic people from all over the world chant "Long live the pope!" It is a nice way for people to say they are happy this pope now leads them and they hope he will live a long life, guiding the church in a kind and openhearted way. Bob did this before he became the pope and plans to continue doing so.

LONG LIVE POPE LEO XIV!

Bibliography

Bunson, Matthew. ***Leo XIV: Portrait of the First American Pope***. Irondale, AL: EWTN Publishing, 2025.

Horowitz, Jason, Julie Bosman, Elizabeth Dias, Ruth Graham, Simon Romero, and Mitra Taj. "Long Drives and Short Homilies: How Father Bob Became Pope Leo." ***New York Times***, May 17, 2025. https://www.nytimes.com/2025/05/17/world/europe/robert-prevost-pope-leo-xiv.html.

"Pope Leo XIV: Mission, Legacy, and the Basilicas of Rome." June 1, 2025. YouTube video, 24:14. https://www.youtube.com/watch?v=oFkeG8lK-jg.

Povoledo, Elisabetta, Jason Horowitz, Emma Bubola, Motoko Rich, and Elizabeth Dias. "Who Is Pope Leo XIV?" ***New York Times***, May 8, 2025. https://www.nytimes.com/2025/05/08/world/europe/who-is-robert-francis-prevost-pope-leo-xiv.html.

TIMELINE

1955 Robert Francis Prevost is born September 14 in Chicago, Illinois

1973 Graduates from St. Augustine Seminary High School in Holland, Michigan

1977 Graduates from Villanova University with a bachelor's degree in mathematics

2001 Elected to head the Order of St. Augustine worldwide

Named the bishop of Chiclayo, Peru — 2015

Becomes a citizen of Peru, holding dual citizenship with the United States

Named a cardinal by Pope Francis — 2023

Elected as the 267th pope in the history of the Catholic Church on May 8 — 2025

WHOHQ